Plane Excitement

By Kurt Blorstad

Odin Publishing

I would like to dedicate this book to all those children, like my grandson, who are born with hemophilia. I have learned more than I ever wanted to about bleeding disorders, but have found the network of families in this community to be the most helpful. Thank you for your support and guidance!

Introduction

Plane Excitement is a collection of short stories based on my experiences while traveling for work. By reading these stories, you will learn a little bit about me and how I see the world. Some of these stories I consider to be funny, some are heartwarming, and others are a little bizarre! I have changed the names of the people I have met during my travels, so if you think you are one of these people, I am sorry to say that you are not. In most cases, this is a good thing because you really would not want to be the subject of one of the more bizarre stories. I hope you enjoy them.

Table of Contents

Table of Contents .... *ii*
The Saint *1*
The Disappearing Arm Trick *5*
Are You Single? *8*
Like A Vacuum *11*
Peanuts or Pretzels *14*
Flower *16*
Because Of You *19*
Yapenstein *21*
The Bunny Hop *23*
The Ups and Downs of Flying *28*
First Class! *32*
Arm Wrestling *37*
A Slight Detour *40*
Trainees *44*
Instructions Required *48*
The Magic Wand *51*
My Thoughts *54*

Diet Snacks	*57*
A NASCAR Pit Crew	*60*
Talks Like An Auctioneer	*63*
My Epiphany!	*67*
It's Raining Vodka	*70*
Please Do Not Spit In My Drink	*74*
Mommy and Daddy and Baby Makes Three	*78*
Flying Should Not Be a Contact Sport	*81*
No, I Am Not Hitting on Your Wife	*84*
Thank You!	*88*
What Everyone Should Know Before Flying	*90*
Acknowledgements	*94*
About the Author	*95*

The Saint

Today's flight started as all good flights should for me - I got on the plane early and selected an aisle seat near the front of the airplane. I have become more tech-savvy from all this flying and for the longer flights, like today's, I download movies to watch. Today's selection was a classic sci-fi B film, *The Adventures of Buckaroo Banzai Across the 8th Dimension*. It has many great actors in it who obviously made a poor choice early in their careers or had the foresight to know that this campy movie would become a cult classic, actors like John Lithgow, Ellen Barkin, Jeff Goldblum, Christopher Lloyd and Peter Weller. There is even a brief appearance by Yakov Smirnoff!

But enough with the movie critique – back to the flight. As other people boarded the plane, a man asked if the seat next to me was taken. I said no and started to get up. He looked at me and said, "No need to get up. I just wanted to save a seat for my wife" and put a bag in the seat beside me.

I said okay and moved the bag over to the window seat since both seats were empty.

He then said, "No, she likes to sit in the middle seat, so would you please move it back."

Now I am thinking, *What does it matter? You are both getting in here, but okay.*

He then put his bag in the overhead bin and sat in the middle seat in the row in front of me as the woman who I assumed was his wife continued walking down the aisle.

I leaned forward to tell the man, "I think your wife left her bag here and chose another seat."

He replied, "Oh, that was not my wife. My wife got a C boarding pass and I wanted to save her a seat up front."

By now, I was thinking that something just wasn't right about the situation so I had to ask. "Excuse me, sir, but why are you not going to sit next to your wife?"

"Well," he stated, "on long flights I like to put my seat back and fall asleep and sometimes I snore, so my wife gently kicks the seat from behind to stop me from snoring. She is so tiny that the reclined seat does not bother her and I am self-conscious about putting the seat back on people I don't know."

I thought, *How do I reply to that? Okay? Your wife is a saint!* Instead I nodded my head and said, "Oh, that's an interesting arrangement."

His wife showed up about eighty people later and

obviously knew to ask me to get up when she saw where her husband was seated. He was correct in that she was a very petite woman. I got up and she sat down. Then I sat back down and said, "If I snore, could you please just nudge me?"

She looked at me and then smacked the seat in front of her. "What did you tell this guy?" she said in a voice that sounded like George Costanza's mother from *Seinfeld*.

"He asked!" replied her husband.

At this point all I could think of was George's parents and I started to laugh on the inside and smile on the outside.

She looked at me and said, "What are you smiling about?"

I said the only thing I could think of – "I'm just happy I am sitting next to you instead of him."

"Well you should be. He snores, uses both armrests, and flops around like a fish when he sleeps. It was my idea to sit behind him and I made up the story about liking the seat in my lap just not to have to sit next to him."

I immediately pulled my arm off the armrest between the two of us and said, "Well, that's great the two of you have an understanding of each other, and it works for you." Then I put in my ear buds and started watching my movie.

Hello, Buckaroo Banzai!

The Disappearing Arm Trick

Sometimes when I travel the fun starts before I even get to the plane. That was the case today. Because I fly often, I am in TSA's precheck program. This means I do not have to take my shoes off or take out the liquids and gels from my toiletries bag, but I still have to remove all metal objects from my person and I go through the metal detector instead of the full body scanner.

As I approached the TSA precheck line – shorter than the others as usual – a woman who was obviously in a hurry went whipping by me and the man in front of me to enter the line. She got to the TSA agent and had her boarding pass pulled up on her phone and her ID ready, but the boarding pass scanner wouldn't read her phone. The agent moved it around trying to get it to register, but it wouldn't.

"I think you need to turn up the brightness on your phone so the scanner can read it," he said to her, handing the phone back so she could adjust it. He waved the man in front of me forward while she adjusted her phone.

"This will only take a second," she said.

"Yes, ma'am," he replied.

As the man in front of me reached the agent, the woman said, "Here, I fixed it." The guard took her phone, put it on the scanner, and it scanned on the first try. He looked at her ID and then let her through. The man in front of me turned and looked at me, rolling his eyes. I smiled and shrugged my shoulders as the woman jogged to the X-ray scanner belt to put her stuff on it. The man in front of me said hi to the gate agent at the same time as the woman walked through the metal detector. It went off. The man in front of me was done and it was my turn with the agent.

As my boarding pass was scanned, I could hear the agent at the metal detector say to the woman, "Go back through and check your pockets. Are you wearing anything metal?"

"NO!" she said, much like my three-year-old grandson when he was being told to pick up his toys.

I put my bag on the belt. The items belonging to the man in front of me had already gone through the X-ray machine and now mine were on their way through. The woman walked through the metal detector again and again it went off. The security guard said, "Ma'am, go back and you will have to go through the full-body scanner."

She said, "I hate that thing!" and thought for a

second. Then her arms disappeared under her shirt. Three seconds later out came what looked like a suit of armor or some type of heavy-duty underwire bra for a knight. She put it in a bin, sent it through the X-ray machine, and walked through the metal detector. No buzz this time.

The man in front of me looked at me and said, "If I had known there was going to be a show, I would have brought refreshments."

I said, "My wife is going to love this story" and I started writing it down as soon as I was through security. After this start to my flight, everything else would seem uneventful.

Are You Single?

Today I am flying, as I often do, and I have a routine for my flights. This flight was no different. I got on the plane, sat in an aisle seat, stowed my stuff under the seat in front of me, adjusted the air vent, and got as comfortable as I possibly could in a seat designed for an anorexic super-model, which I am not.

As the plane filled up, a woman asked if the seat next to me was taken. I said no and got up to let her in. She sat down in the middle seat between me and another man and said, "Man, this menopause is killing me. I am so hot." Then she proceeded to grab all three air vents, turn them on full blast, and point them at herself. I waited a few seconds, then started to reach up to readjust my vent and got a look that said, "If you touch that vent I will bite your arm off." I stopped mid-reach and slowly lowered my arm back by my side. As much as I would have liked to have a little cool air, I was not reaching up to reposition that vent. Somehow, women everywhere would know if I did and hold it against me.

As the flight progressed, she decided the other man next to her should not be reading the book he brought with him and instead should be talking to her. She told him all about her entire family and their lives. At this point I had my earbuds in and was pretending to listen to music, but I was really listening to her story and to the other man's responses. He kept trying to be polite and end the conversation by saying, "Oh, that's nice" every time she paused and opening his book to start reading again, but this did not stop her. She told him about her four daughters and what they did, how she motivated them all through college, and that she was the reason they all graduated. She talked more about one daughter in particular, saying that she was still single and should settle down with someone nice.

Then it hit me! *She thinks this guy would be a perfect match for her daughter.* As I listened, I heard all the clues. She continued to talk about Amanda and how she was into fashion and more of a homebody than the others. I do not think the guy understood, but I was laughing on the inside as hard as I could without letting on. I often sit near people who have tried hitting on the other person next to them, but this was the first time I've seen a mother hitting on someone for her daughter.

Well fortunately for this young man it was a short flight. I do not think he was able to read even one page of his book, but the spine managed to get a good workout. She talked to him all the way up the Jetway and it was not until he excused himself to go to the men's room and said goodbye to her that they were split up. I was not sure if she was going to follow him in or wait for him to come back out, but I was behind schedule and continued past them. I am sure he spent a long time in there before he came back out.

Like A Vacuum

Today's flight started like most usually do with my normal pre-takeoff routine. As the plane started to fill up, a woman sat in front of me with a pair of dollar-store reindeer antlers on her head. She was giving out candy canes to all the remaining passengers boarding the plane. Most people took one and said thank you or Merry Christmas and moved on. It was a great diversion because I still had the empty center seat next to me and she was like a shield of sugar blocking their view. This was great!

I looked up and did not see anyone else boarding the plane. *Maybe that's everyone. I think I am going to have some extra room on this flight. Woo-hoo! Maybe this is the airline's Christmas present to me.*

Now relaxing in my seat and a half, the woman in my row started the usual polite conversation that most people have prior to taxi and takeoff. She told me about her job and that she travels a lot, blah blah blah. She said she had an extra drink coupon and asked if I would like to use it. I told her I didn't drink and thanked her for the offer. Just then another person got on the plane. *Don't look. Avoid eye contact. Cough like I'm sick*. I tried all the usual ploys hoping one of them would work.

As the passenger walked towards where I was sitting, the flight attendant said, "Take the first seat you see as there are only middle seats left." I looked up and our eyes met.

"I don't fly well and I was running late," she said. "I didn't have time to go to the bathroom and I forgot to take my Valium, Dramamine, whatever and I don't like being touched - I mean being in contact with other people while I am sitting."

I started to get up and as I did I looked at the woman in the window seat. She looked like she had seen a ghost. I know she was thinking, *Don't let that crazy woman sit next to me!* and I know she wanted me to slide over, but I didn't. I got up and the crazy woman sat in the middle seat.

The woman in the window seat was now pressed up against the window like a vacuum was sucking her against the side of the plane. I sat back down, leaning into the aisle so as to not touch the crazy woman. She sat there tapping her fingers and looking in the seatback pocket for the airsickness bag.

The woman in the window seat pulled out a slip of paper. "Here, I have this extra drink coupon. I think you need it more than I do!"

I thought, *If the crazy lady doesn't take her up*

on her offer, she is going to use both of them.

The rest of the flight went okay after they both got their drinks, but I spent the entire flight hanging out in the aisle, getting bumped by the flight attendants and people going to the bathroom. The crazy woman seemed relaxed and never got up to use the bathroom. Looking back, I think she said all that to try to get me to move over so she could have the aisle seat. The things people will say to a perfect stranger.

Peanuts or Pretzels

Today's flight started like any good flight should – it boarded on time and the plane was only two-thirds full so when we took off, I had an empty seat next to me. This is a rare occurrence on the airline I fly and I am sure if they could figure out how to charge passengers for the empty seats beside them, they would. Since there was nothing interesting happening right next to me, on this flight I would have to expand my search area to write today's story.

I looked around to see the normal number of gray-haired people for a flight coming from Florida. Some of them were reading books while others were engaged in polite conversation with people they may have just met. Others, like the guy in my row, were trying to sleep.

Then it was food service time.

Now when I was younger and flew, the food was served by nice young women in heels with a smile who would give you a tray of food. It might have been a sandwich with some fruit or a salad and a cookie or if it was a dinner flight, maybe meatloaf, mashed potatoes, a salad, and a cookie. Not any more though! Now some old guy might hand you a cookie if you were lucky, but most likely you just got a small bag of pretzels or peanuts. There is a slogan on the peanut bag that says, "Your flight is so cheap that it only cost peanuts." Well, if it only costs peanuts, you should have a lot more of them to give out than just this tiny bag with about ten in it!

I think all the airlines secretly have a pool going to see who can give out the least amount of food. It probably goes something like this:

"Hey! Bob, what did you give out today?"

"Well, I gave out small bags of pretzels with only 15 pretzels in each."

"Okay, that's good. Gary, how about you?"

"I gave out bags of Mini Lorna Doones with only 13 cookies in them."

"Wow! That's great!"

Then Mark speaks up. "I can beat that. I had peanuts to give out and then I told everyone that there was a kid with a peanut allergy on board, so I apologized and only gave out the drinks."

"Oh man, that was a great idea! You win this week's pool. Okay, everyone put in money for next week and remember that you can't use the same trick twice."

Flower

Today's flight took me to Rochester, New York where the high was a lovely 22 degrees. This flight had many passengers on it that came from Fort Lauderdale, Florida and continued with me to Rochester. Given the number of passengers already on board as this was a continuing flight, I had to sit back a little farther than I usually do from the front of the plane, but I still managed to get an aisle seat.

As the plane filled, a young mother with her baby asked if the seat between me and another man was spoken for. Normally this is the kiss of death because a screaming child is most passengers' worst nightmare, but I have become more understanding since the birth of my grandson, Connor, 18 months ago. I replied that it was not spoken for and got up to let her in.

It was a very windy day and as the plane taxied towards the runway, it rocked slightly. Some of the passengers had distressed looks on their faces and were fidgety, but not the little girl sitting next to me on her mom's lap. For the rest of this story, I will call her Flower because she had a small flower in her hair which made her even cuter, if that was possible. Unlike most of the adults around her, Flower must have found this rocking soothing because she had a big smile on her face.

Then I heard, "We have been cleared for takeoff." The plane turned, faced down the runway, and started speeding up.

As soon as the wheels left the ground, the plane quickly yawed to the left from the strong crosswind and then climbed, shuddering and creaking as it ascended. A few seconds later, one of the overhead compartments near the front of the plane popped open. For the next few minutes, the ascent was more like a rollercoaster ride with many passengers holding the arms of their seats with a firm grip and concerned looks on their faces. Then there was another abrupt yaw and pitch change with that dropping elevator feeling.

Some passengers made sounds of concern, but not Flower. She just put her arms out to her side and said, "Uh oh" with a large smile on her face. I laughed out loud as she seemed to be enjoying what the other passengers did not. For most of the flight, Flower played with her mom and a little toy that lit up and made sounds. She was very content with the tight quarters and would occasionally lean back in her mother's lap with her sippy cup in one hand, a pretzel in the other, and a look on her face that said, "Man, can life get any better than this?"

The landing was a little rougher than the takeoff, but Flower remained unfazed. She stretched, then yawned, and was now nearly asleep. Flower is by far the best passenger I have had the honor of sitting next to. I wish all passengers were so content.

Because Of You

I was running late and just managed to board the plane in time. I was very lucky because it was only half full so there was plenty of room to spread out. I got an aisle seat near the rear of the plane. This was a very uneventful flight – no crazy woman, no people with interesting stories, just a very smooth flight. Normally I would not write about this type of flight, but it is what happened after I landed that was important to me.

As I exited the plane and walked up the Jetway, a small group of men stood just past the end of it. When I got closer to them, I saw they were all wearing WWII Veterans hats and remembered that it was Veteran's Day. As I approached the first man, I put out my hand to shake his and say thank you! He looked at me, smiled, and shook my hand. I proceeded through the group, shaking their hand and thanking them one at a time for serving their country. As I got to the last man in the group, he shook my hand as the ones before him did, but asked, "Why are you thanking us?"

I replied, "Well, first of all, I am thanking you for serving our country, but mostly I am thanking you because without people like you I would not be alive." He had a confused look on his face, so I explained. "My father grew up in occupied Norway during World War II and if men like all of you had not defeated the Germans, then my father would not have been allowed to come to the United States and meet my mother. So, in a roundabout way, because of you and others like you I am here to shake your hands."

He smiled. "Well okay, you're welcome."

Later that day, I emailed the airline I frequently use to ask them if they would set up a charity to fly surviving WWII veterans to Washington, DC to visit their memorial. If it was possible, I wanted to be the first to donate the majority of my frequent flyer points. In their reply, they said that they could not set up an account themselves and that it would have to set up by the people who would be using the account. I then emailed the WWII Veterans website at ww2.vet.org, but have not heard back yet. I will post updates to this story on kurtblorstad.com as information becomes available. Happy Veteran's Day!

Yapenstein

It was a snowy day across the northeast when I boarded the plane today and I was the first to sit in my row, allowing me to get the aisle seat. As the plane filled, I was joined by a young newlywed couple with their lap dog in tow. Now I know most newly married couples are strapped for cash, but if it were my honeymoon, I would have found a relative to take him or asked for dog-sitting as a wedding gift rather than bring him along.

He was placed in a small, soft travel case under the seat and I could see his beady little eyes looking out through the mesh at me. He was quiet until the plane started moving and then he began making a little yapping sound. The bride next to me made a shushing sound and the dog quieted down. But when the plane revved up the engines to takeoff, the engines must have been making a sound that only dogs could hear and it was one this dog obviously did not like. He was now yapping continuously and to me the sound was worse than fingernails on a chalkboard. The lovely bride apologized and said, "I have never seen him act like this before."

I replied, "Do you mean the dog or your husband?"

She turned her head and looked at her husband who was now asleep, obviously tired from too much honeymoon. She then turned back to me and said, "Both of them."

I thought, *The honeymoon is over*, but was smart enough not to say it out loud.

The bride reached under the seat and pulled Yapenstein out to console him. At that moment, the plane's engines revved down and that must have made the dog whistle sound disappear. All I know is that annoying yapping had come to an end. Now Yapenstein was as quiet as a mouse. He was a little cuter then I imagined, especially since there were not any bolts coming out of his neck. Tito, whose real name I had just learned, was a Mexican hairless. He was now getting his belly scratched and was stretching his neck and kicking his legs while panting with enjoyment. Then he went back into his travel case for what would be a very quiet rest of the flight.

As the plane landed, Tito made one more little yelp as if to say, "It's about time."

This also woke up the groom, who said, "Well, that was an easy flight." I laughed on the inside and his wife just shook her head and smiled.

The Bunny Hop

As I arrived at Baltimore/Washington International Thurgood Marshall Airport, I noticed very long lines outside for the baggage check which meant the lines inside were even longer. Not good, especially since it was only 45 degrees outside. I also noticed a large number of families and what looked like a pack of twelve-year-olds traveling together, but I am sure they were college students. Then it hit me – it must be spring break since today was April 2nd. I walked inside and saw that the security checkpoint lines were just as bad as those at baggage check. Even the TSA pre-check line was a five-minute wait; on a normal day, it was less than a minute.

Since I had to wait, I figured I might as well do what I always do at airports – people watch. Now, the attire of today's travelers varied from heavy coats to shorts and t-shirts. You could tell the people who were on vacation and heading somewhere warmer – they were the ones in shorts and t-shirts. They must have wanted to make sure they got that vacation experience for as long as possible. Some of these people, I believe, changed their clothes in their cars as they left work or school the day before in an effort to extend their vacation and would probably change their clothes back on their way to work or school when they returned.

When I walk through any airport and I am not in a hurry, I like to look at people to read their different stress levels and guess what category they might fall into. I currently have three categories for airport travelers: the "Huffers" are in a hurry and every little thing that slows them down seems to make them huff and puff in disgust. The "Zombies" are clueless to what is going on around them and seem to have plenty of time to get where they are going. They are never in a hurry and are the group that causes the Huffers the most stress. Then there is "Everyone Else." Everyone Else is aware of their surroundings, very polite and respectful of others, and not in a hurry unless faced with a dilemma or something unexpected.

Such was the mom of the little girl in the bunny ears and puffy tail sitting across from me while waiting to get on the plane. The little girl's bunny costume was very cute, not at all like the one Ralphie wears in *A Christmas Story*. The mom definitely fell into the Everyone Else category.

Or she did, that is, until her little girl in the bunny costume realized "Nina's got to go!"

Now if you have small children or grandchildren, you know what that means. If not, you soon will know.

As the little girl was hopping around moments

before, her mother asked many times if she needed to use the bathroom and explained that they would soon be getting on the plane.

"No, Mommy, I am just practicing my bunny hop," she replied. Five minutes later, as if a little light went off in her head, "Mommy, I need to go!"

Now in her defense, if I had been hopping around as much as she had, I would have had to go, too, but that's another story.

After hearing her daughter, the mother quickly went from Everyone Else to a Huffer! She grabbed her daughter and their bags and dashed to the bathroom, which, fortunately, was directly across from where we were sitting. As they got up, the gate attendant announced it was time to board the plane. Everyone got up and stood in their numbered positions.

A few minutes later, we started to board the plane. As I headed to the Jetway, I saw no sign of Nina or her mom. I boarded the plane and got my usual seat with two empty seats next to me. As the boarding process continued, several people looked at me and then smiled and proceeded on down the aisle as if I had the plague. On the airline I am flying today, the passengers get to choose their own seats. This often makes me self-conscious when there are only single seats left in every row. I wonder what people are thinking as they pass one seat up for another. Am I taking up too much room and maybe they will feel cramped? Am I scary looking or do I smell bad? I do shower and dress nicely as not to scare people off, but today I guess that was not enough. Then! At the front of the plane I saw bunny ears. Nina must have broken a world record in the ladies' room because she and her mom were now heading down the aisle. Her mom looked like she must have bent over to help Nina and ended up having a bad experience with the hand dryer because her hair was – well, let's just say it was a little disorganized. As luck would have it, Nina and her mom asked to sit next to me to which I said, "Well of course. It would be an honor to sit next to the Easter Bunny."

Nina looked at me and said, "I am not the Easter Bunny. I am Kelly and I am three and a half." She held up three and four fingers alternating to show me her age in case I did not hear her. Kelly got in first and sat in the middle seat.

Her mom said, "Move over, dear," and Kelly looked at her mom and smiled. Her mom then just climbed over her and sat at the window. Kelly's mom looked at me and asked, "You don't mind if she sits next to you, do you?"

"Of course not," I replied, knowing darn well that I had brought this on myself. From the time we took off until the time we landed, Kelly showed me what she brought with her in her Peter Cottontail backpack and explained how the

Easter Bunny will find you even if you go to your grandma's house for the week. *The last thing this little girl needs is more sugar*, I thought as I listened to her talk a mile a minute. *Let's hope her Easter candy is sugar free.*

When the plane landed and stopped at the Jetway, everyone got up and started to exit the plane. As I stood to get my bag out of the overhead Kelly tapped me on the leg, reached in her backpack, and handed me a sticker of a bunny. I thanked her and said, "I am sure that the Easter Bunny will have something special for you for being so nice." Her mom looked at me and smiled while nodding in agreement. I took my newly acquired sticker and placed it on my shirt and headed off the plane. When I got to the top of the ramp, I stopped to make a phone call and saw Kelly and her mom zip by me towards the bathroom. Nina's got to go!!

The Ups and Downs of Flying

Today is a beautiful day to fly. It is sunny and 71 degrees with little to no wind. The only issue is that I would be leaving that nice weather for Buffalo, New York where it was the exact opposite – cloudy, windy, and 17 degrees. To make matters worse, they were expecting snow! And of course, the snow was not expected to come before we landed so there was no chance of us being diverted somewhere else like Bermuda.

It was time to board the plane and if you have read enough of these you know where I sat – yes, that's right, in an aisle seat near the front. This time I was quickly joined by an older couple on their way to visit their daughter. After the wife took her seat next to me, she started going through her bag, pulled out some things, and then decided to put her bag in the overhead compartment. I got up and offered to do it for her. Fortunately, there was still space in the overhead compartment, so I put it in and sat back down.

Today's flight looked to be full. I could only hope that most of these people leaving Florida had been on vacation or were going to visit people like the older couple sitting next to me, because Buffalo would not be my first choice to visit in

January if it were not for work sending me there. As we prepared to leave the gate, the flight attendants started their spiel. When they got to "all phones must be turned off or in airplane mode," the wife turned and said, "I am sorry, but my phone is in my bag and I forgot to turn it off." So I got up, opened the overhead compartment, got her bag, and handed it to her.

Her husband said, "Now you know why I sat by the window." She smacked him and then pulled out her phone and turned it off. After she handed me back her bag, I put it back in the overhead compartment and sat down once again.

We finally took off and when we got to altitude, the pilot turned off the fasten seatbelt sign. Then the wife tapped me on the shoulder and said, "I need to get up and use the little girl's room."

I replied, "I think this plane only has little boys' rooms on it." She looked at me, paused, and then laughed. I got up to let her out and then I sat back down. As she walked to the front of the plane, the flight attendant said, "Sorry, ma'am, the restroom is occupied and you are not allowed to wait at the front of the airplane. Please go back to your seat and wait or use the restroom at the rear of the plane."

I quickly looked to the rear of the plane and saw a line of three people for that bathroom. As she turned and started to walk back, I knew she was going to sit back down and wait for the front restroom to become available so I slid over to the middle seat and turned to her husband and said, "Hello, Dear." He smiled, which was maybe a little scary. Then she sat in my seat and waited for the bathroom to become available.

When the person in the front restroom came out, she got up and went to the restroom, and then a few minutes later she came back. I got up again. She sat down and then I sat down uhhhhhgain. I thought maybe from now on I should choose a window seat, but wait! Not even ten minutes later, her husband had to get up to use the bathroom.

REALLY!! Was I looking a little too comfortable for you or is this how you get your wife to exercise! We all got up. He got out and his wife sat back down and then I sat back down one more time. He was gone for a while. By the time he returned, the captain had turned on the fasten seatbelt sign in preparation for landing. When I got up to let him back to his seat and before I sat down for what I hoped would be the last time on this flight, I asked his wife if she needed anything out of her bag or wanted me to put anything away while I was up and she said, "Yes."

I pulled her bag down from the overhead and handed it to her. She said "Thank you" and reached into her bag and pulled out her phone and handed the bag back to me to put back in the overhead. She turned to her husband and said, "As soon as we land, I want to be able to call our daughter so she can pick us up.

I wonder how many times her daughter will have to stop the car on the drive home for her mom to get something out of the trunk or use the bathroom.

The plane finally landed and I got up to get my bag. When I handed the woman her bag she said, "Thank you" and as I walked off the plane I realized that so many interesting things seem to happen to me when I fly that I should be writing them down and, even though this is not the first story, it is the one that inspired me to start writing things down.

First Class!

On today's flight I got bumped up to first class. For me this is like winning the lottery – not like the Mega Millions, but more like winning $500 on a scratch-off ticket. Since today's flight is a long coast-to-coast flight, the extra room will be a welcomed comfort. Normally I would get an aisle seat so that I could spread out a little more when the aisle isn't being used, but they gave me a window seat. I am sure this will not be an issue with all the extra room you get in first class.

A flight attendant greets me as I walk down the jetway and when I enter the aircraft, I am amazed. There were 20 seats in a space that fits 42 further back. As I quickly do the math, I wonder why these seats cost three to four times as much as general seating, but that's a discussion for another day. I walk up three more steps and I am there. My row! There are only two seats! And there are pillows and blankets on every seat! And look! Between the seats there is a console with drinks and snacks! There is so much room! When I have had to walk through first class on previous flights I did not notice all this stuff. This must be why first class passengers get on first – so they can hide all the good stuff before the regular passengers get on.

At this point I realize I am holding up the boarding process and quickly store my bag in the overhead storage bin that is reserved for first class passengers and grab my iPad and briefcase to sit down. You would think that with all the extra room in the row navigating a single aisle seat to get to the window seat would be easy and maybe the seasoned first class passenger has this mastered, but that is not the case for me. As I step into the row I manage to knock all the prizes and extras that they put out for us onto the floor. Not wanting to step on all of the items I reach over to put my briefcase and iPad on my seat. The pillows and blankets on the seats are wrapped in plastic so when I place my stuff on top of them they slide off the seat onto the floor with the rest of the items. With all the issues I am having, I feel and look like Dick Van Dyke when he walks in his front door and trips over the ottoman.

I lumber around for a second and manage to get all the items picked up and put back and sit in my seat. After a deep breath I survey my surroundings and notice there is enough room for all my stuff and the complimentary items they have left for me, as well as a small TV screen and numerous pockets in the seat back in front of me, but no tray table. Instead of being on the seat back, the table is in the large console between the seats and folds out when you need to use it.

By this point, most of the first class passengers are on board and seated. The flight attendants come around and offer us drinks while the other passengers are still boarding. I have too much stuff already – where am I going to put a drink! I realize some of the items have to go. The other passengers boarding are now at a standstill as they wait for people to take their seats and I notice a little girl with a Minnie Mouse backpack standing in the aisle with her mother. I turn and grab my wrapped pillow and blanket and say, "Excuse me, you are the 100th passenger to board the plane and you have won a free pillow and blanket." She now has a huge smile on her face and she and her mom both say thank you at the same time. For me it was an easy choice. She is the only one small enough to have room for a pillow and blanket in the tight seats at the rear of the plane and since I am a grandfather I now appreciate a warm smile more than anything else.

When the boarding process is complete and we prepare for takeoff, the flight attendants come and pick up the now finished drinks. The normal preflight safety spiel is displayed on the TV screen in front of me and a recording is played over the loud speakers rather than being acted out as a live performance. I only mention this because when they get to the life vest portion they say that the life vest is under your seat in a pouch, but if you are in first class they are in a CASE under your seat and on the screen they show you how to open it. Why a case? Is mine gold-plated and needing to be locked up?

The plane heads down the runway and lifts off. As we ascend the flight attendants come around with hot towels. I am not sure why, but I guess maybe if you stirred your Bloody Mary with your finger, you may want to clean up a bit. After towel time they came around for food service where they take a second set of drink orders and ask what you would like for breakfast.

Breakfast! I get breakfast, too?

The choices today are a red pepper omelet with fruit and a yogurt cup or an everything bagel, oatmeal with cinnamon and raisins, and some fruit. I had eaten breakfast not knowing I would be getting a meal so I say no thanks and just ask for water. The lady next to me orders the omelet meal and a coffee. She then pulls her tray table from the console and the flight attendant brings a mini linen tablecloth, places it on her tray table, places the meal on the tablecloth, and hands her a linen napkin with silverware. This is not the same airline food from the '70s and '80s. I am usually not a fan of red peppers, but this meal looks and smells really good!

After breakfast they come around several times to offer us more drinks and some light snacks. They also offer free earbuds to use with the TV. Not wanting to waste all this extra space and comfort I decide to take a nap. I must have fallen right asleep because the next thing I know the flight attendant is tapping me on the shoulder to say that I need to put my seat in its upright position in preparation for landing.

Overall this was a great experience, but the issue is that now I know what I will be missing as I walk past the first class area. Maybe that was the airline's plan all along and they upgraded my flight hoping I will upgrade on my own in the future. Well, maybe I will if my wife is traveling with me – she deserves the first class experience, too.

Arm Wrestling

Traffic was miserable. I thought I had left in plenty of time for the drive out of town, but traffic, especially in Atlanta, Georgia, can be a PAIN IN THE- ...let's just say it's unpredictable. Returning the rental car, I am sure, was as timely as usual, but when you are rushed it seems like it takes forever. I got through security quickly and as I headed to my gate I heard my name over the loudspeaker. "Paging Kurt Blorstad. The cabin doors are about to close and you will not be allowed to board the airplane once they close. Please proceed immediately to gate B-12 to board your flight." This is not what I wanted to hear. The only time I want to hear my name over a loudspeaker is when they are announcing lottery winners.

After running for what seemed like an hour, but was probably only two minutes, I managed to make it to the gate before they closed the door. Walking down the Jetway I prepared for the reality that there was no way I would get an aisle seat and I suspected I would be sitting near the rear of the plane. As I headed down the aisle, I managed to find room for my baggage in an overhead compartment and a little farther back I found a seat in the last row. Of course it was between two men who were bigger than my 6'2",

200 lb. body. They looked no happier to see me than I felt to see them.

I squeezed in.

I know, because I am one, that men often believe that we deserve both armrests and then some. It took my wife to point this out to me and ever since then, when I sit next to the smarter sex (not these two men), I make a point NOT to use both armrests and to be as considerate as possible to all the passengers who fly any of the flights on this Sardine Wedged Airline. As I settled in for the flight, it was obvious that these two men had never met my wife!

Six arms and four armrests – well, you do the math. There were no armrests left when I sat down. I am not sure how the guy sitting in the aisle seat managed to get the one between the two of us, but he must have gotten up and sat back down without his arm ever leaving the armrest. *Hey! I guess that means the stewardess didn't goose me when she squeezed by the two of us in the aisle? It was that man's arm!*

Anyway, I sat in my seat trying to plan my armrest attack. Given that it was a short flight from Atlanta to Baltimore, I knew that neither of the men would be getting up to use the bathroom so my only chance would be beverage time. When they reached up to get their drinks, I would be able to get at least one armrest and then I would use the other hand to get my drink when it comes. When the flight attendant got to our row, the guy by the window was asleep. I ordered water and the guy at the aisle said, "No thanks, I don't need anything."

Okay, time for plan B. When my drink comes, maybe he will hand it to me if I pretend to be busy. The flight attendant finally got to our row with my drink. As I reached up to put my tray table down, the guy on my right who was asleep slumped down and his arm came well past the armrest into my seat. I turned to get my drink and the stewardess must have had Gumby arms because she had reached all the way over and set my drink down on my tray table without even leaning over. So the *B* in plan B was for Bad Idea because I had lost ground in the battle for armrest space. These men were obviously pros in the armrest game and I, the seasoned traveler, had been outwitted by both of them.

When the Sardine Wedged Airline flight came to an end, it felt good to get up and stretch. From now on, I make sure to allow just a few more minutes to get to the airport – the fate of my legroom and armrests depend on it.

A Slight Detour

Today was a beautiful day in Tampa, Florida, but like all good business trips, it eventually came to an end. It was now time to fly home. I arrived at the airport with enough time to eat before my 4:00 pm flight. After eating, I boarded the plane, which was about forty percent full, and got my usual seat location near the front and on the aisle. Prior to closing the door, the flight attendant came on and said, "This flight is being detoured to Fort Lauderdale and then it will continue non-stop to Baltimore."

This did not sit well with the woman in front of me. She got up and approached the flight attendant asking, "What do you mean detoured? Why are we going to Fort Lauderdale first? I have a connecting flight. Are you going to hold that flight? There is no f-ing way I am going to miss my connecting flight." She was obviously having a bad day and this was the last straw. Before the flight attendant could utter a response, the woman had already gathered up her stuff and was heading up the aisle demanding to get off.

The flight attendant said, "Ma'am, there is no need for language like that. Please sit back down."

I thought, *LET HER OFF!* As I watched, I was surprised that the woman had not been sitting next to me – I'm usually a magnet for people like this.

The woman said, "No," and at that point security had obviously been called. They entered the plane and one escorted her off.

The flight attendant talked to the other security guard who must have given the flight attendant the woman's name. She looked it up and said to the guard, "No, she did not check any baggage."

The guard said, "Then you should be good to go." So we taxied and took off.

It was a short flight to Fort Lauderdale. As we arrived at the gate, the flight attendant said, "We will try to make this a quick turnaround, so please stay seated."

The first to come aboard was an older couple who obviously needed assistance to board the plane. A young woman got out of her seat in the first row and moved to a seat farther back in the plane. Her seat, plus the empty seat that had been next to her, made room for the older couple to sit together and they were very grateful. The plane filled quickly with people who looked like they had not slept in hours or even had a chance to freshen up, including the man asking to sit next to me. Once he took his seat I turned to him. "Excuse me, sir. They diverted our flight to come to Fort Lauderdale. Do you know why?"

He nodded. "Well most of us were on a flight to Baltimore that should have left at 8:00 am, but when we were on the plane a thunderstorm came and delayed our departure. So we sat at the gate for about two hours. When that was over and I thought we were getting ready to leave, the pilot came on and said there was a minor mechanical issue and that maintenance was coming to fix it, but after two more hours, they said that we would all be getting off to board another plane. So we all got off and were reissued new boarding passes and then walked to another gate to board the other plane." He paused before continuing.

"We were all on board the second plane and just getting settled in when the flight attendant announced that the flight crew we had was now off because they worked the flight down and were only allowed to work so many hours a day. They had reached that amount, but were contacting other flight crews to take their place. After an hour, they told us they were going to let us off the plane to be more comfortable and they would be giving us new boarding passes – again! So we got off to find large containers of drinks and snacks at the end of the Jetway with them telling us that there were no flight crews available for us and they would have to rebook us on other flights."

"Well as you can imagine, there was a rush to the ticketing agents. By this time it was 3:00 pm and there were a lot of people and very few flights left with seats. With all the complaining and irate passengers, they finally told us they were bringing in another plane and it would be landing around 5:00 pm. When they got on the speaker and told us your flight had landed, I was skeptical whether it would actually make it to the gate and leave on time, but I am glad it has."

I said, "Man, that is a crazy story! I thought what happened on my way here was crazy, but your day was even worse. You have had enough issues today and you don't need me telling you what happened on my way here." I was right. He had fallen asleep while I was talking to him. The rest of the flight was uneventful because most of the passengers were asleep from their long day.

Trainees

I was running late once again and missed my boarding group, but did manage to get an aisle seat three rows from the back of the plane with the other two seats still empty. The flight was maybe two-thirds full, but I was soon joined by two older women (old is a relative term, but I would guess they were in their early seventies). I guess these were the only two seats together left on the plane, so they had no choice but to sit next to me. Judging by their colorful clothing, they were making their annual migration south from Buffalo, New York where we were to Fort Lauderdale, Florida where the plane was heading. This was not a direct flight for them and I would be getting off in Baltimore, Maryland, the first stop on the flight.

As we left the gate, the flight attendants started their spiel. I should have noticed the women's college team all in matching sweat suits seated in the midsection of the plane when I first boarded, but I noticed them soon enough. They had obviously flown too many times together and had now decided to help the flight attendants with their spiel.

They all had the flight safety information cards held above their heads and flipped them around in unison with the flight attendants. Then as the flight attendants said to fasten our seat belts low and across our lap, they all managed to fasten theirs at the same time which made the clicking sound very pronounced. When the attendants mentioned the emergency exits, they all had two fingers on both hands pointing forward, then to the rear, and then to the over wing exits and finally the young women seated in the aisle pointed to the pathway lighting.

At this point, the announcing flight attendant mentioned that there were twenty-plus trainees on board to help today and in case of an emergency not to listen to them, but to listen to the actual attendants assigned to this flight. She then continued with, "Should there be a change in cabin pressure, four oxygen masks will drop from overhead." At that point, all the female athletes pulled out what looked like the elastic band a nurse puts around your arm to draw blood. They all held up one end and snapped it, then covered their mouths with their hands while the flight attendant said to breathe normally. All at the same time, they took two deep breaths with their mouths covered, which sounded like twenty-plus Darth Vaders. *Sheeee Hooooo Sheeee Hooooo.* They high-fived each other, laughing.

I believe the flight attendants did not wish to be outdone so as the plane left the ground and entered that steep climb, one of the flight attendants made an announcement. "Would all the trainee flight attendants please prepare for food service?" With that, the flight attendant at the nose of the plane started sliding the snacks down towards the rear of the plane. With the steep incline the plane was on, things went by quickly. The women athletes were caught off guard and maybe had not put their best players in the aisle seats. The flight attendant up front counted as she slid items down the aisle and the flight attendant at the rear counted what made it all the way to the back of the plane. When the inflight entertainment ended there was an announcement – the final score was experienced flight attendants: six, trainees: four. Another victory for the experienced flight attendants.

Zola and Judy, the two ladies seated next to me, looked like deer caught in headlights. This was obviously more than they were used to seeing on their flight. Judy leaned over to me and said, "Are they allowed to do that?"

I replied, "Well, on my last flight, the passengers caught the food as it came down the aisle and threw it back at the flight attendants."

Judy said, "Really!"

I said, "No, I am just kidding. They really gave each passenger a free drink if they were lucky enough to grab something as it went by."

"Oh! I don't think those college girls are old enough to drink. They could get in trouble if they do that," said Judy.

"I am sure they will check their ID," I said.

Zola and Judy talked the rest of the flight to each other as I tried to relax. Mostly they discussed who they were going to visit first when they arrived, when their family would be coming down to see them, who would get a bed, and who would sleep on the fold out. Oh and that Judy's son-in-law snored and he was loud so he would get the back bedroom. The rest of the short flight passed quickly and as I got up to get off the plane, I told Zola and Judy to have a good time in Florida. Then Judy, with a surprised look on her face said, "What, you're not coming with us?"

I smiled and said, "Sorry, if I was given more notice, I would have been able to squeeze in a visit." I took a step, then turned back and said, "But not when your son-in-law is down. Loud snoring keeps me awake." They smiled and wished me well. So ended another flight to remember.

Instructions Required

Just when I think there couldn't be anything else to write about, I have a day like today. While boarding the plane, a man in front of me was on a phone call. He was talking loudly as he waited in line, as he made his way down the Jetway, and as he was putting his bag in the overhead compartment. As much as modern technology is a good thing, way too many people don't know when it is *not*. This man was one of them.

I knew by listening to his conversation, as many of us on the flight were whether we wanted to or not, that this was not as important a phone call as he seemed to think it was. It could have waited until we landed or better yet, been handled with an email. Instead, everyone around us had to listen to him as he talked.

When he finally took his seat, I went four more rows back before I chose mine. I tried to be far enough away not to hear him at full volume, but not so far back that it would take me an hour to get off the plane. As I sat down, I realized that maybe this man was smarter then I gave him credit for. Many people try different things to deter people from sitting next to them such as spreading out so if you thought of sitting next to them, you would be cramped. Or they cough a lot so you think they are sick when they really are not. Maybe this annoying phone call was a new ploy and once everyone sat down, he would still have an empty seat next to him. If that was his plan, it worked. There was an empty seat between him and another woman as the door was secured.

As the flight attendant started her spiel, he finished his call. I can imagine I wasn't the only one who was relieved. There was an eerie quiet now that his loud conversation had ended and there was a brief moment when no one was talking at all. The plane took off and we got through most of the flight before that changed. As we started our descent, I heard him talking again. I knew he could not possibly be on the phone, but soon realized that he was using one of many voiceover Wi-Fi apps that allow you to talk to anyone, anytime, if you have an Internet connection. This flight had Wi-Fi and these types of apps were not yet blocked.

Five minutes into his conversation, a woman's voice rang out. "WILL YOU PLEASE JUST SHUT UP! Are you unaware of all these other people around you and that we do not need to be witnesses to your conversation?"

I could not see who said this, but I was pretty sure it was not the woman next to him because he turned around to look for who said it. I applaud this woman for saying what most people were thinking.

He quickly said, "I have got to go. I seem to be annoying the people around me."

He ended the call and the flight sounded like a library once again as we continued our descent. There were no awkward moments as people got off the plane, but as I left the Jetway and proceeded to get my luggage, everyone started to spread out and I heard several suggestions for flight etiquette and what they would have said had that woman had not spoken up first. Modern technology is wonderful, but it really needs to come with instructions for some people.

The Magic Wand

I was glad to be traveling because it was bitter cold in the northeast and I was headed to Miami, Florida, but I wished my wife would tag along more often on trips like these. I travel so much that I miss her company and a little getaway time is good for us, as I'm sure it is for all couples. The occasional return home to the welcoming "Well hello, stranger" has its advantages, but as I get older I find comfort in knowing there is someone out there who actually wants me around, as quirky as I am. Our evening phone calls are good to catch up, but they are not a good replacement for a face-to-face conversation. Okay, enough of that.

As I boarded the plane and got to my seat, a businessman and who I later learned was his assistant, Joan, started to claim seats near me.

He was on the phone, saying, "Yes, Joan has all that with her."

As he spoke Joan was saying, "No! All of that is back at the office." Hoping they did not hear her comment he continued to reassure the person he was talking to that he had everything under control.

They both sat down in aisle seats with him in front of her. I am fairly sure she wanted no part of sitting next to him. He then turned around to her and said, "I'm going to put my seat back during the flight. You are okay with that, aren't you?" This was like him saying, "If you are not okay with this, then move now and take your chances elsewhere and I will annoy someone I don't know." She decided to stay and deal with the devil she knew rather than taking her chances somewhere else.

As the plane filled up, a man with a hard case bag that obviously would not fit in the overhead compartment asked if the seats next to me were taken. I said no and got up. He tried to get his bag in the compartment above the businessman across from me. He put it in handle first and tried to close the door. It did not close. Joan commented, "It's too big. It's not going to fit." He then pulled out the bag, turned it around, and put it in wheels first. It was still hanging out. Joan again said, "It's too big, it's not going to fit." Now her boss, tired of having this man over him, offered to help.

I thought, *Unless you have a saw, this bag is not going to fit in the amount of space left in that bin.* He got out of his seat and I noticed he was probably only five feet tall. He got up and stood on both armrests on either side of the aisle and started pulling the bag out and forcing it back in, over and over again. I guess he was either trying to dent the outside of the aircraft or hoping to compact the bag some so it would fit. It did not work. He then rearranged other bags in order to make space to turn this bag sideways.

The whole time, Joan was saying, "It's not going to fit." By then the people waiting in the aisle were all offering suggestions, some not so nice.

Finally, the flight attendant came and said, "I will get that for you, sir. Please take your seat and let the other passengers get by." Now I kind of missed the next step, but I think the flight attendant waved a magic wand and all the bags moved. Then she turned the bag sideways and closed and latched the door.

Joan just shook her head in disbelief and said, "I never would have thought it would fit in there."

Her boss said, "I almost had it when she asked me to let the other passengers get by."

I am just glad the bagman did not make a hole in the side of the plane.

My Thoughts

Here are some things you may hear from the flight crew or flight attendants prior to takeoff along with my take on what they say:

- "Here at Southwest, we do things a little different." – *Yes by charging me for the chance of getting a decent seat! Maybe you should assign boarding passes when people book their flight. Reward those who plan ahead and not those who have no life and can be on five computers trying to log in exactly 24 hours before their flight.*
- "Here at Southwest we have an open seating policy, so when you board the plane please select any seat you would like." – *They seem to frown at me asking to sit next to the pilot or in one of the fold-down seats meant for the flight attendants. The open seating policy is also a bad thing for women traveling alone since it leaves them vulnerable to that sleazy man who thinks all women want him and somehow he is going to get lucky during the flight or once we land. I see this often and I am always amazed at how superficial some men think women are.*

- "In the case of a loss in cabin pressure..." – *...the manly man trying to pick up the woman in seat 36D will most likely panic and grab all four air masks, making the other two passengers in his row hold their breath.*
- "In the case of a loss in cabin pressure, four air masks will drop down from overhead. Please put your mask on first before assisting..." – *...your screaming, childlike husband.*
- Or what I hope never happens in the row I am sitting in. "In the case of a loss in cabin pressure, four air masks will drop from overhead..." – *so please do not all grab the same one.*
- "In the case of a water emergency..." – *...and this flight should become a submarine...* – "...there are life vests under your seats for flotation."
- Or my favorite. "In the case of a water emergency..." – *...and had we had prior knowledge this was going to happen, this flight crew would have called in sick and you would be seeing the backup flight attendants all in bathing suits.*
- "If you are sitting in an exit row and do not wish to perform the duties required of sitting there, please tell us and we will relocate you to another seat." – *Really? Who does not want to be right by the door when there is an issue? Who is going to say, oh yes! Please, put me as far*

from all the exits as possible so when there is an issue, I can sit back and finish my peanuts before it is my turn to exit the burning aircraft. A famous comedian once said, "That's okay; when the plane crashes, I will just go out the big gaping hole in the side of the aircraft."

As announcements go, it doesn't get any worse. Except for "Oh, look, a squirrel!" Okay, you're not going to hear that even if your plane crashes in a tree, but who wants to think about the alternative announcement?

Diet Snacks

I really did not want to leave Miami. It was sunny and 70 degrees there and back home it was not! At home, it was ten degrees. I boarded the plane and once again sat in the front in an aisle seat. The plane filled and I was joined by a young man and woman who were traveling for business together. They had come down for training, but managed to squeeze in some partying and relaxation. The young woman was focusing heavily on her coffee and trying to open a bag of Reese's Pieces. It got the best of her for a good five minutes before she decided she just had to use the bathroom before we took off. I guess that being frustrated by a sealed bag must have induced a bladder response in her. We got up to let her out and she headed against traffic, like a salmon, to the bathroom at the front of the aircraft as the other passengers boarded the aircraft.

When she came back, she looked confused and said to her traveling companion, "I think we are on the wrong plane. While I was in the bathroom, I heard them say we are going to Austin."

I looked her straight in the eye and replied, "Yes, this plane is headed to Austin."

Her jaw dropped and then she said to her co-worker, "We are on the wrong plane."

I said, "Why is that? Where are you headed?"

"To Baltimore," she replied.

"Well, this flight stops in Baltimore on its way to Austin," I replied.

She looked at me, frowned, and then said, "Isn't Austin in Texas?"

"Yes, it is in Texas," I said.

Her co-worker and I got up to let her in as she said, "I will try to only get up one more time and, if you're lucky, I will fall asleep and not need to get up at all." With that she took out her contacts and put on her glasses and attacked the Reese's Pieces once again. Given the effort she was putting in, they may have been diet Reese's Pieces since she burned more calories trying to get into the bag than were actually in the bag itself. This time, with her glasses on and an empty bladder, she completed the task in less than three minutes. After consuming her Reese's Pieces, she fell asleep for about an hour and a half.

When she woke up, she needed to use the bathroom once again. I can only imagine that she was dreaming about trying to open a bag of Reese's Pieces and lost the battle. While asleep, she often changed positions and I thought I heard her mumbling, "Chocolate, peanut butter, chocolate, NO peanut butter" right before she woke up. Well, the flight ended without incident and we left the plane with a polite goodbye, saying "Have a good weekend" to each other. I was just glad there weren't any more candy casualties.

A NASCAR Pit Crew

Before we boarded today's flight there was a lot of line chatter as we all stood in our numbered positions waiting to board the plane. I overheard the people in front of me talking about how there used to be more flight options to Rochester before this airline merged with another and that those choices of flight times were a lot more convenient for business travelers. Then the woman in front of me said she was not a fan of the boarding process and that people who get on first should sit in the rear of the plane so boarding would be quicker. She also complained that the standing room between the numbered pylons was not big enough for five skinny models, let alone five normal sized people.

Now this woman was maybe 5 feet tall and might have weighed 100 lbs. only after visiting an all-you-can-eat buffet so I am not sure whether she was hinting that we were all a little too close to her or if the mirror she owned at home was one of those funhouse mirrors that made you look taller and wider.

"I often thought the same thing, but figured if I said that out loud to someone, every woman in line who heard me would take offense to my opinion and think I was calling them fat," I told her.

I think at that point she thought about what she had said and replied, "No, no, no, I didn't mean that the people in this line are all fat. I was just saying that, well you know, that not everyone is the same size and... well... you know what I mean."

I didn't respond.

We boarded the plane and needless to say, she did not sit next to me. Instead, I was joined by three different generations of women - a grandmother, her daughter, and her one-year-old granddaughter, Molly.

Molly was as cute as can be with a little pink bow in her hair. She was very outgoing and liked to smile and laugh. She was also very curious and wanted to touch everything, including me. She offered me her pacifier, her rabbit, and her book on three different occasions and was obviously teething as she chewed on anything she was holding.

Partway through the flight Molly's mother decided that a wardrobe change was needed, most likely because of the smell coming from Molly and the fact that the front of her current outfit was wet with drool. As the plane was ascending and the fasten seat belt sign was still lit, the two adults got to work with the speed of a NASCAR pit crew. At one point I even thought I heard the distinct *zip, zip, zip* of car tires being changed, but it was just Molly enjoying her wardrobe change. The process was quick and odorless (thankfully) and Molly came out of the pit rejuvenated with her arms racing a hundred miles an hour. Her mother played a quick game of Pat-A-Cake with her and then pulled an iPad out of her bag and put it on a game where Molly touched items that each made a sound. When Molly heard the sound, she would clap. This kept her occupied for the remainder of the hour-long flight. Molly may not have been Flower, but she's right up there with her as a great travel companion.

Talks Like An Auctioneer

Some days I just get tired of all the traveling. This was one of those days. Still, I do my best to be polite to those nervous flyers who just have to talk to someone to help keep their minds off of their pending flights. I am usually eager to share the details of my life such as what I do for work, what my kids do for work, and the fact that I have a grandson. If they also have grandchildren, this usually means we are close in age.

Because this was one of those days where I was so tired, I decided to change what I do for a living in hopes that my "job" would hinder conversation and allow me to relax on the flight. As the plane filled up, an older couple asked to sit next to me, so I got up to let them in.

They said thank you and sat down and then the man introduced himself. "Hi, I'm Howard." I told him my name and he continued, "And this is my wife, Angela." After I said hello to her as well, the two of them started talking to each other.

Angela pulled the *Sky Mall* magazine out of the seat-back pocket and started browsing, commenting on all the unique items she found to Howard. This went on through the taxi, takeoff, and the first half of the flight and then suddenly, almost in mid-sentence, there was silence.

Angela had fallen asleep with the magazine in her lap and her head against the side of the plane. As I listened to the silence I thought, *Now that the shopping critique has ended I may be able to nap.*

Well of course not! Howard obviously needed someone to talk to or, from what I gathered over the last forty minutes, he more likely needed someone to listen to.

He asked me why I was headed to Miami. It was the perfect first question.

"I am traveling for work," I replied, then sat back and waited for him to ask, "Oh and what do you do?" Instead he said, "I used to travel a lot for work also and have recently retired and I am using my frequent flyer miles to take my wife places she has never been. This is our first trip together since I retired. She does not fly much, so I figured to get her to fly I would entice her with some place warm during the winter. So we are headed to Key West. We are going to drive from Miami to Key West because I do not think I can get her on a small plane. The drive is about three to four hours, but we are going to stay for a month with a friend. So the long drive will not be an issue for her. I know she will love it there when we arrive." He spoke very quickly and never seemed to stop to breathe.

"She likes to shop and sit on the beach. I like to people watch. There are lots of crazy people in

Key West. Have you ever been there?"

"No, I have no—," I started to answer.

"Oh, if you like the beach you would love it there. It is very relaxing. No one is in a hurry."

Now I thought to myself, *Anyone who has to listen to this man talk ninety miles an hour is not going to be relaxed.*

Howard continued on. "It hardly ever rains this time of year and the water is warm and clear. I think I will take Angela on a sunset cruise. It is very relaxing just going slowly around the island watching the sun set."

He continued talking for the next twenty minutes and I quickly learned that this man did not need someone to listen to, he just needed someone to talk to – or in this case – talk at. I had no chance to talk about the job I did not do in an effort to detour conversation so I could relax. So I made a break for the bathroom even though I did not need to go.

As I got up, Howard decided it was a good time for him to do the same thing. So he nudged his wife to let her know where he was going. *Really? If she woke up and did not see you, will she panic and think you jumped off the plane?*

I headed to the bathroom at the front and Howard headed to the one to the rear.

I did my fake business, enjoying the cramped, but quiet, room. I washed my hands just because it was a bathroom and that is what I do. I headed back and saw Howard as he came up the aisle. He sat down first.

Lucky for me, Angela had not fallen back asleep and was again commenting on the unique items in the magazine. Howard was quiet and spit out an occasional "oh that is neat" or "that's nice" and I got to relax for the last fifteen minutes of the flight. Maybe next time when I am tired and flying I can use the "what I do not really do for work" deterrent because there was no chance to get even a word in edgewise on this flight.

My Epiphany!

For some reason, I decided to fly out early. I usually take a 9:00 am flight, but this flight left at 6:50 am. From where I live this meant I had to wake up at 4:30 am to get to the airport on time. This is not a good time for me. I like my sleep. I used to have a job where getting up at 4:30 am was a daily occurrence and it was one of the many reasons why I changed jobs.

The only advantage of flying earlier was the lack of traffic heading to the airport, but the time I saved on the drive was lost when I arrived at the security checkpoint. It turns out I wasn't alone in my planning and a lot of people think that this is a great time to travel. I have never seen a line this long at security since right after 9/11. Everyone on the road with me must have also been going to this airport.

Eventually I got through security and boarded the plane. I sat in seat 4C and was quickly joined by a man who seemed a little stiff and not very mobile. He got in and stood at the middle seat. So I asked, "Are you waiting for someone?"

He said, "Yes, my wife."

I sat down while he stood next to me waiting for his wife.

"I would sit down, but if I do it is hard for me to get back up," he told me. "Originally, we got C 21 and 22 for boarding passes, but I decided to pay for an A boarding pass so we could sit together. I did not want to pay for two A boarding passes and figured I could save her a seat, so we only purchased one pass."

I said, "That was a very smart thing to do."

Because his wife was the next to last person to board the plane, he stood crouched over for a good fifteen minutes talking to me. I was starting to think that maybe she should have gotten on first and saved a seat for him, allowing him to be a little more comfortable.

When she arrived, her husband and I got out of our seats, let her into the row, and we all sat down. Throughout the process, he had raised both armrests and I thought it was to make it easier for his wife to get in, which would have been very nice of him. But when I sat back down and tried to put the armrest down between us, he said, "Oh, I would prefer if the armrest could stay up. Is that okay?"

I see this as a polite way of saying, "I plan on using my seat and your seat and it would be a lot easier without the armrest in my way." Even though I did not like the idea, I decided to be polite and agree.

Neither of them were larger than the small

amount of space given to you on an airplane, but the husband did manage to sit on about ten percent of my seat with his wife lying at an angle cuddled up next to him trying to sleep using her seat and about twenty-five percent of his seat. I guess she also did not like getting up early and wanted to catch up on her sleep on our way to Fort Lauderdale.

After about an hour, he decided to get up and use the restroom and stretch his legs. This woke his wife up who felt bad that he got up, so she apologized and decided to tell me his life story.

As she told me his story, I began to relax. The heart issues and blood clots this man had reminded me of the ones my father had before he passed away from cancer. It is amazing how interacting with people helps all the little inconveniences seem to not really matter anymore. At this point I decided, rather than complain or think negatively of a situation, I would first try to get some perspective and understand that not everyone's life is as good as I believe mine to be.

It's Raining Vodka

All the interesting things I write about seem to happen on flights from Fort Lauderdale to Baltimore. This flight in particular was full of interesting people. It started as my flights usual do, with me in an aisle seat seven rows back. First there was a couple where both individuals wanted to sit in aisle seats. The man sat in front of me and his wife sat across the aisle from me since the rows did not line up. I have noticed this seating arrangement more and more as I travel. I am not sure why couples do not sit together. When I travel with my wife, we take turns sitting in the center seat. My wife takes more turns than I do, but I still offer.

Next a young woman sat in the center seat across the aisle from me. She was saving the window seat for her boyfriend, who was about ten people behind her in the boarding process. When he reached her row, the woman in the aisle got up but the young woman stayed seated and made her boyfriend climb across her. Because he was a larger individual, he decided to do this face to face in an effort to keep his backside out of her face. Unfortunately he tripped and fell as he made his way into the row, landing in a position that I am sure can be found in the *Kama Sutra*, the ancient Hindu text on human sexual behavior. She laughed aloud hysterically, he moaned, and I commented that they were supposed to do that before they got on the airplane. The people behind them laughed as the boyfriend tried to free himself from being wedged between the seat and his girlfriend.

After the couple managed to get separated and into their seats, another couple walked up and asked if the seats beside me were taken. I said no and got up to let them into the row. After they sat down, the two began talking and I overheard him ask her, "Did you remember to take your airsickness medicine?"

I pulled out my airsick bag, handed it to her, and said, "If you had told me about this issue first, I would have said the seats were taken." Her boyfriend laughed and it was quickly apparent that this was probably not a smart thing for him to do. The woman looked at him with that look all women use to non-verbally say, "That was stupid of you and you will regret it later on."

As more passengers boarded the plane, a man got on and asked to sit in the middle seat in the row in front of me. He tried to put his bag in the overhead compartment and had to rearrange all the bags that were already up there to make enough space. Determined to make his bag fit, he grouped some of the smaller soft bags together and shoved them all to one end of the compartment to get his in. As he moved things around, I heard a sound like glass breaking and it was clear that the gentleman heard it as well. He paused for a second, quickly closed the compartment, and sat down.

Eventually we took off without any other issues. About an hour into the flight, I could smell the faint scent of alcohol, but assumed that since the flights attendants were serving drinks the aroma was coming from them.

I was wrong.

Not ten minutes later, something started dripping from the overhead compartment onto the man in front of me in the center seat, the same one who had rearranged the items in the compartment moments earlier. After a few more drips landed on him, he got up from his seat, opened the compartment, and said, "CRAP! I think I broke my vodka bottle." And yes, he now had luggage that was wet and smelled like vodka.

Fortunately for me, my bag was in the next overhead compartment and was unharmed. The people who had their bags in the same compartment as his were not so happy, thinking that their bags might also smell like vodka. It turned out that his bag had taken most of the damage and the bottle did not break completely, it was only cracked and leaking. He removed it from his bag and had the flight attendant throw it away. The man next to him asked how he got it through security as you cannot even get a water bottle through without security taking it and he said that he bought it at the airport in New Orleans before his flight to Fort Lauderdale.

After the initial disgust and nerves, everyone sharing the overhead bin with him decided there was not as much damage to their belongings as they originally thought. I was surprised, but maybe the aroma of alcohol was making everyone more agreeable. The rest of the flight went well and we soon landed. As we walked off the plane, one of the wheelchair attendants on the Jetway did comment, "Man! You all smell like you had a good time on that flight." So ended another eventful journey home.

Please Do Not Spit In My Drink

Today I got an early boarding pass and managed to get an aisle seat in the exit row where there is a little more leg room and the seats in front of you cannot be reclined. That is a huge thing for me. I usually get a good boarding number, but most of my flights are continuations, so the few people left after the de-boarding tend to relocate to the better seats. It took a long time for everyone to board the plane because there were two teenage girls' lacrosse teams with their chaperones and coaches on this flight. Most sat in the back and then finally they filled in the center seats throughout the plane. My row only had two seats available and none of the teenage girls were old enough to sit there, so they asked for a volunteer to move with one of the mothers saying she would. Like so many flights before, I wondered why it takes so long to fill the seat next to me on a full flight.

Once everyone was seated, the flight attendant came to us and asked, "Do you all know that you are sitting in an exit row and are you willing to help in the event of an emergency?"

The woman next to me rolled her eyes and said, "Yes, I know. You just asked me to sit here." The flight attendant then asked her to put her bag under the seat before continuing with her spiel.

Then the flight crew closed the doors to the aircraft and asked all the passengers to put their devices in airplane mode. The woman next to me pulled out her bag and turned her phone off, just as the flight attendant walked by and said, "Ma'am, you need to put your bag completely under the seat in front of you." The woman looked at her as if to say, *I am not a child! I know what to do.*

It seemed obvious to me that she had been spending too much time with the kids she was chaperoning – she was acting more like a rude teenager than the actual teenagers on the plane. She mumbled something under her breath and then pushed the bag under the seat with her foot. All was going well until they came around to take drink orders. When the flight attendant came to our row, the woman ordered a Bloody Mary made in a way I have never heard of before. The flight attendant said, "Yes, I can do that," and must have looked down, because she asked the woman to put her bag under the seat in front of her. I had been busy playing a game on my iPad so I'm not sure when or how it was moved, but when I looked, there it was, right by her feet in the aisle again.

As I watched the verbal and non-verbal exchanges between the woman and flight attendant I thought, *She is going to spit in this woman's Bloody Mary.* So to let her know I was not with this woman, when she asked what I would like I smiled and said as politely as I could, "Just water if it is not too much trouble." She smiled and I felt sure my drink would be fine.

When she delivered the drinks, I said, "Thank you," but the woman next to me said nothing. She took her drink and then held it because her tray table was not down. The flight attendants then came around with snacks. One asked if I would like something and I said yes. She handed me some chips and some peanuts. She then asked the woman next to me if she would like any snacks and received a grunted "yes" in response.

The flight attendant put the woman's snacks on my tray table on the side closest to her, since her tray table was *still* in the upright position and she was holding an almost empty drink in one hand and her phone in the other hand playing a game.

They both need a drink and I need to be seated somewhere else in case one of these women goes postal!

The flight continued on and soon started its descent. As we prepared to land, the flight attendant announced over the intercom that all large items must be stowed and the seat and tray tables put in their full and upright position. When I saw the flight attendant coming down the aisle I kindly told the woman next to me that she may want to push her bag back under the seat in front of her.

It turns out that was not a good idea.

By this point she had now decided that the whole plane had turned against her. "I know what I have to do and do not need everyone telling me!" she mumbled.

I said, "Sorry, I was just trying to—"

And before I could finish she gave me the stink eye, put her earbuds in, and that was that. So now I have learned what not to do again in the future and started feeling sorry for her family. I can only imagine what her friends and family had to listen to when she got home and shared the story about her flight.

Mommy and Daddy and Baby Makes Three

Today was a beautiful day in Baltimore for it being August and as I headed to the airport, I knew the weather in Miami was 95 degrees and humid, with a chance of rain. I didn't want to go, but I guess if I have to go to Miami every two weeks throughout the year, I should be happy that for most of the winter in Miami it is 75 degrees when in Baltimore it is 30 degrees. That thought helped a bit.

I arrived at the airport and everything went smoothly. I had an A17 boarding pass and was able to get on the plane early enough to get an aisle seat in the fourth row. As usual, the middle seat between me and another passenger remained open even though the plane seemed to be completely boarded. Today was looking like a good day for traveling – I would have some extra room to spread out and relax. If only one or two seats remain empty on an entire plane, about 20 percent of the time I am lucky enough to have one of them next to me.

Just as I was planning my relaxation, a young couple with a six-month-old baby in tow boarded the plane. The mother got to where I was sitting and asked if she could have the seat next to me. I of course said yes and got up. She sat down and I sat down and the husband continued down the aisle carrying their son. At first I was relieved that I was not next to the parent with a lap child, but then after about two minutes, it hit me. I turned to the mother next to me and asked if her husband had anything to carry on other than their son. She looked at me confused and answered nope he did not. I could see she had the diaper bag under her seat and knew this was not a good sign of things to come. So I asked her if she would like to sit with her husband. She turned her head and with a big smile said, "That would be great!" I picked up my stuff and headed to the rear of the plane to find her husband and son sitting, surprisingly, in an aisle seat two rows from the bathroom. I was surprised about the aisle seat, not the bathroom.

When I asked him if he would like to change seats and take mine so he could sit next to his wife, he looked relieved and said thanks more times than I could count as he got up. He quickly headed to join his wife.

I sat down and was now seated next to two boys. I would guess they were about ten and twelve years old with their parents seated behind them.

As I settled into my new seat, one of the flight attendants, Cathy, came by and asked why I changed seats with the man. I said, "Well, his wife was sitting next to me up front and it took me a minute to think back to when I was traveling with small children and how hard it was when we could not sit together. Since I was alone, the five extra minutes it will take me to get off the plane is nothing compared to what I hoped would make their flight easier."

She reached into her pocket and handed me a drink coupon. I thanked her and put the coupon in my bag. I do not drink, so I planned to give it to someone on a future flight. When the plane landed and I finally got off, the young couple was still at the end of the Jetway trying to organize their stroller with all their other bags. As I passed, they said thank you again and I handed them my drink coupon and said, "You're welcome and one of you might want to use this for the return flight." As I walked away I thought to myself, *I hope the one that uses this is not their baby.*

Flying Should Not Be a Contact Sport

Sometimes when I board the plane and get my usual seat, I think I am invisible. At least that was the case today as the majority of the passengers who squeezed down the aisle all seemed to come in contact with me as they went by. I don't mind the occasional bump by the little kid who is more excited about being on the plane than anything else and is just not sure how the rolling backpack should be navigated down the aisle. It is the people who are just not paying attention as they head to their seat that bother me. Add to that the fact that the aisle is so narrow and the majority of the male population, including me, are wider than the space provided. This is not a good design and with space at a premium I do not see this changing anytime soon. When I board I do my best to head down the aisle doing the side step while holding my bags sideways to keep them from hitting things or people as I head to my seat. When I get to my seat, I make sure to look around me for clearances from other people before attempting to stow my bag in the overhead compartment. You'd think that backpacks would help solve this problem since they remain behind you as you walk down the center aisle, but when you turn, your backpack still remains behind you and it swings into the seat that your back is to. Unfortunately, not everyone realizes this.

On this flight in particular, there were ten people with backpacks. Six of them sat in the seats across the aisle from me. None of them knew how to turn into a seat while wearing a backpack. Normally when I see the backpackers coming, I lean into the seat next to me, but the seat next to me already had someone in it and I am fairly sure the nice woman next to me did not need my head on her shoulder, so I took one – or as luck would have it, six – for the team.

Unfortunately, it was a one-man team - me!! I think I caught the woman next to me laughing while covering her mouth at my repeated beatings by the backpack brigade. I felt like I was playing a game of Whack-A-Mole and I was the mole.

Then, as if the backpacks weren't enough of a beating, when the man who went to sit behind me was putting his bag up over my seat, he realized it was not going to fit and pulled it back out. He was not able to control it and it fell to the floor, but only after my head slowed down its decent to my arm and then to the floor. I asked him if he needed help with his bag because I now felt like part of his luggage.

He replied, "Oh, did my bag hit you as I was getting it down?

No, I am rubbing the knot on my head with my left arm because my right arm is still numb, I thought to myself. I stood up and managed to smile through the pain as I helped him with his bag. I put it far enough away from me so that the next time it was removed it would not hit me again.

After the boarding process, the in-the-air portion of the flight went well. Thankfully the people who were doing a majority of the lifting and carrying, the flight attendants, are masters at carrying drinks and snacks down the small aisles without bumping into anyone.

When we landed and got to the gate, I stood with everyone else to get ready to get off the plane. The backpack brigade somehow had all managed to get out of their seats and stand up as I did and had all somehow maneuvered their positions to surround me. They were all swinging their backpacks around their shoulders to their backs to reattach them. Yes, I saw this coming and tried to maneuver back into my seat, but was too late. I leaned in as far as I could while not being obtrusive, but to no avail. Two of them managed to whack me. The woman now half in my seat could see my expression and smiled and said, "It is just not your day, is it?"

I replied, "No, it is not. From now on I will be getting a window seat when I fly." Flying should not be a contact sport.

No, I Am Not Hitting on Your Wife

Today I am flying on Airbus A320 operated by Delta Airlines. It has a beautiful cabin with redesigned overhead bin storage that holds a lot more than the older planes. It also seems to make walking down the aisle easier for me. This is a relatively new airline for me to fly on and so far I am impressed. They have more seating options than my normal airline and have a first class section, of which I cannot afford to fly in. They also have a section with extra legroom. It is the four rows right behind the first class seats. Since I am 6'2" my company will pay for extra legroom on longer flights and I appreciate this very much.

On today's flight I have a window seat with extra legroom. When I go to sit down there is a gentleman in the aisle seat and I tell him I am in this row. He looks at me and scrunches up as if to say, "Please climb over me." Now this row has extra legroom, but not enough for my 200 lb. body to pass his 210 lb. body while seated. From my point of view this is obvious, but maybe not to him from a seated position. I tell him I would appreciate it if he would get up to make my journey to the window easier and he reluctantly obliges me. As he stands, I realize I should not work at a carnival guessing weights because I'm pretty sure my estimate was wrong and I feel bad for asking him to get up. As I sit down he is still standing, talking to the lady in the aisle seat across from him and I am now sure that she is his wife. Either that or he calls everyone "dear."

After speaking with his wife he sits back in his seat and passengers continue boarding the plane. A few minutes later a young girl stops and tells the man at the aisle seat in my row that she has the middle seat. Again I should not be guessing ages either as she looks to be 15. For me this really means she is probably 25. This time the man quickly gets up to let her in and then sits right back down.

As the plane fills up there are still two empty seats next to this man's wife in the row across the aisle from us. The flight attendants close the door and get ready to depart, confirming that there are no more passengers left to board the plane. The wife of the man in my row says to her husband, "Would you like to come sit with me? There will be an extra seat between us for more room." He thinks quickly and says, "No, I really like the aisle seat."

I can't believe my ears! Really? The two of you like each other enough to travel together, but always want to be three feet apart? In addition to his declining to join her, she could have offered to move over herself and give him the aisle seat, but she didn't.

I am not a shy person so I lean forward and ask the man if I could sit with his wife. He looks at me with a look that says "No way!," but says nothing. His wife leans forward with a confused look on her face so I clarify myself and say to him, "I won't actually sit next to her, I will leave the empty seat between us so we can all have some extra room."

I notice the girl next to me smiling and trying not to laugh, but even with my explanation I get another confused look from the man. All I can think of is he thinks I am hitting on his wife, of which that is not the case at all. I am just trying to make this three-hour flight a little more comfortable. So I think quickly and then say, "Maybe this young lady between us would like to have a little more room. I am sure she would rather have an empty seat next to her than have to sit between two large men." This seemed to make sense to him. The young lady looks at me with a big smile on her face and says, "Thank you!" as he gets up to let her out. She moves to the window seat on the other side of the plane and we all sit down.

As we resettle into our seats, the man turns to me and says, "It is going to be nice to have some extra room to spread out on this flight." All I could do was say, "Yes, it will be nice to have the extra room" while biting my tongue. I cannot imagine the day will come when I would rather sit in an aisle seat next to people I don't know rather than sit in a middle seat next to my wife. I know they say people who are married get comfortable with each other as they get older and if what they have works for them, great! I just hope I am never that comfortable.

Thank You!

If you have enjoyed reading these stories and have received this book for free, I hope that you will make a donation to The National Hemophilia Foundation by going to their website and their donation page. Please fill in Plane Excitement as the tribute name. Next put your name on one of the lines below and then give this book to someone who will enjoy it. If you are lucky enough to fill in the last available line then this book is yours to keep and there will be a prize for one lucky owner of a book so please check my website for an update.

Thank you for your support!

_____

_____

_____

_____

What Everyone Should Know Before Flying

When flying, today's travelers seem to forget (or perhaps they just do not realize) that they will be in a very confined space for several hours. It is not just the time in the air that you need to consider, but also the taxiing, takeoff, landing, boarding, deplaning, the ground stoppages, weather delays, and redirections to another airport. With all of these considerations, here are some tips for traveling by air:

Food: Bring an extra snack and a bottle of water or drink for weather delays or unexpected parking of the plane on the Tarmac so you do not go hungry. This is also handy during a rough flight where the flight attendants are not allowed to get up for their safety and cannot do the snack and beverage service. Keep in mind that there are very few flights where you actually get a full, or even a small, meal. However, if you do choose to bring your own meal, please make sure it does not have a strong smell. You may really want that great tasting sandwich with onions and garlic or that delicious tuna fish sandwich you bought in the food court, but remember you're not the only one on the flight. When you bring foods with a strong aroma, everyone on the plane will have to smell it for several hours. When this happens in the lunchroom at work, I have the option of politely getting up and leaving. If I stand up on a plane and say, "Does anyone want to change seats with me that likes the smell of tuna fish?" the person next to me might be offended. Please dine with consideration.

Pets: Now I know that airlines are trying to be more accommodating and small pets that fit under the seat in front of you are acceptable, but please try to make sure they have been recently bathed and fed prior to traveling. A smelly dog is not the best traveling companion. Most people bring treats for their dogs to help them relax should they start barking or whimpering because they are nervous or sensitive to the pressure change, but, unlike the man I sat next to recently, a bowl of moist canned dog food is not what you should be feeding your dog.

Travelers with service animals should get to choose any seat they want. On most flights, I have noticed they do get the very first row where there is room for the service animal to lie down. I also think that if needed, they should be given a second seat for free so the service animal does not feel crowded. After all, service animals are often larger dogs.

Children: For those families traveling with children, you really need to plan ahead. What you need to plan for varies widely with the ages of your children. While it would not be my first choice, I believe kids ages ten and up are just plug-and-play and can be easily kept occupied while traveling with any video game to play or show to watch. When my kids were that age back in the 1990s, Apple was not what it is today with all their small personal electronics so we played cards and hangman or they would read a book as I perused the cool new things in the *Sky Mall* magazine. Lap children are also generally not an issue if you have prepared for the pressure change that may cause them discomfort. There are many good articles and posts online from experts on what to do such as breastfeeding or making sure they are using a pacifier or bottle during altitude changes, but make sure they are not lying down when doing this. There is also a slightly more aggressive solution calling for acetaminophen or ibuprofen, but please check with a doctor before choosing this option. It's the three to nine year olds who seem to have all the energy. While being in a confined space next to someone they do not know seems to calm some of these kids, it makes others more rambunctious. When my kids were this age my solution was to leave them at home with my in-laws – this way my wife and I would get to relax more while on vacation.

I wish I had some better suggestions, but don't bring children with you unless it's necessary. If possible, take the money you would have spent on them to travel and give it to your in-laws or whoever is watching them to spend on them while you are away. You, your kids, and your fellow passengers will be happier for it.

Armrests: We all know that unless you fly first or business class, you are not going to get two armrests. I believe that if you are in a row with three seats (and as you know, there are only four armrests with these three seats) the person stuck in the middle should get the use of two of them.

Under-seat storage: I am not sure why, but even though the seats we sit in are evenly spaced, it seems the storage under the seats in front of you is not. The aisle seat has the smallest amount of space in front of it for storage and the center seat has the most. The window seat varies depending on whether you sit near the front because that is where the plane narrows. Although they still manage to get three seats in there, the head room and leg room is restricted by the ever-shrinking diameter of the plane as you move closer to the nose where the pilots are seated. Plan accordingly.

Your stories: If you have a funny or interesting story from a recent flight and would like to share it, please visit kurtblorstad.com and tell me about it. I will post the most interesting ones I receive.

Acknowledgements

I would first like to thank my wife for all of her help and for putting up with me during this endeavor. I would also like to thank author Jeff Gunhus for his help and encouragement, but mostly for being honest with his criticism on what he thought should change and for recommending others to talk to for help, including Sheryl Hartwell. She along with Krista Sennett reviewed my rough stories and then taught me about timeline consistency and how a short story should flow. Of course there were also the numerous spelling and grammar corrections they helped with. The final editing was done by Diana Morris and I really appreciate that she took the time to explain her thought process and viewpoint. She made several suggestions on adding and deleting lines or passages, but left it up to me for a final decision. I recommend them to everyone I talk to. Lastly there is a large group of people who helped me with setting up and testing the website along with trial downloads of the book - thank you all! Without you the launch of the book would have been a mess.

About the Author

I have been told by many people that I tell a good story and so my first book is just that: me telling what I believe to be the most interesting stories of people I've met and events I've experienced during my many travels for work. I have found it a lot harder to tell these stories through the written word than it was to sit on the couch and say to my wife, "Guess what happened on my flight today!" I should have spent more time in high school listening to my English teachers rather than flirting with Barbara Billerbeck. Fortunately, I have some very supportive friends and relatives who were willing to help me. I had three people read my work and correct my grammar even before I felt comfortable enough to send it to a professional to edit. I talked to a prospective editor several times before she could work me into her schedule. I think offering her a bonus of good Norwegian dark chocolate helped win her over. That or she just wanted to put a stop to my relentless calling and emailing.

Now that I have been bitten by the writing bug and my first short book is about to be published, I have started working on two other books (yes, sometimes I have an issue staying focused on one project at a time). First, I started working on *Growing Up Me*, a book about my time in elementary school from 1967 to 1974. My second (or technically, third) book comes from the monthly visits with my Uncle Olaf and our numerous conversations about his youth. Taking the stories he's shared, I decided to write a book about my father's family and their struggles during the German occupation of Norway. My father passed away 10 years ago, but between all the stories he told me about his youth and my talks with Uncle Olaf and Aunt Thelma, his brother and sister, I've become aware of how hard it was for them. *Occupied* will be the story of their struggles.

The goal of my writing, at the very least, is to leave my children with a sense of what it was like for their parents and grandparents to grow up when they did. Perhaps that will inspire them to write about their own lives one day and keep this going as a family tradition.

A portion of the proceeds generated from my first book, *Plane Excitement,* will be given to foundations dedicated to helping those with hemophilia and other bleeding disorders. My daughter is a carrier of hemophilia and my grandson is a hemophiliac. They are lucky enough to have good insurance, but there are many others out there who are not so fortunate. To kick this off, I have made my first book free to download and at the end of the book, I provide links to either the National Hemophilia Foundation or the Hemophilia Federation of America's websites for you to make a direct donation.

Thank you for reading it and thank you for donating!

Kurt Blorstad

www.ingramcontent.com/pod-product-compliance
Lightning Source LLC
Chambersburg PA
CBHW070530030426
42337CB00016B/2171